Edited by Jan Colbert and Ann McMillan Harms

With photographs by Ernest C. Withers and Roy Cajero

Dear Dr. King

Letters from Today's Children to Dr. Martin Luther King, Jr.

Hyperion Books for Children

New York

Acknowledgments

From the moment Melanie Colbert first broached the idea of this book, until the time David Colbert ensured it had a safe haven, we have had the backing of many talented people. Family, friends, and colleagues listened to the letters and to our ever-evolving vision of what this book should be.

We are indebted to the educators and students at the following Memphis City Schools for their support:

Caldwell Elementary	John P. Freeman School
Campus School	Grahamwood Elementary
Denver Elementary	Sea Isle Elementary
Douglass Elementary	White Station Elementary

From our first general meeting with the principal of White Station Elementary to the last parental permission form tracked down by a dedicated teacher at Caldwell Elementary, the willingness to add to their already full schedule served as a constant reminder of what education is all about. We were moved by the extent to which the students had been taught (and what they remembered!) about Dr. King's life and work. The letters showed us that his legacy is alive in these schools, full of a rainbow of children who are being inspired every day to achieve their dreams.

HOW THIS BOOK CAME TO BE

As parents and educators, we've seen the story of Martin Luther King, Jr.'s, life and work take root in the hearts and minds of children. That's especially true in this city, Memphis, Tennessee, where his life was tragically cut short.

This book grew from discussions with school principals and teachers, parents and children. As Dr. King came alive again, through study and reading, we encouraged a group of Memphis teachers to suggest their students write letters to him, posing questions or telling about their own lives and feelings, their perceptions of the past, or dreams for the future.

What amazed us most was how comfortable the children felt in writing to Dr. King. Clearly, the faith of grandparents who marched with him, parents who continue to share his ideals, and teachers who tell of his life and legacy has been firmly instilled in this new generation.

The letters poured in, and we spent months reading and rereading many times more letters than could be included in a single volume. We were continually overwhelmed by the eloquence of the children and the depth of their concerns.

Ernest Withers generously shared hours with us in his studio, bringing his photos to life with the heart and wit of his reminiscences. Roy Cajero's pictures mirror his feeling for the project and his innate ability to capture the children at just the right moment. Wycliffe Smith transformed the parts into a wonderful whole we could never have imagined. Their enthusiasm helped fuel our own.

As we laughed and cried over the letters, it was the conviction we heard in the children's voices that moved us most. It is these children who will grow up to be the generation to transform all of Dr. King's dreams into reality.

—Jan Colbert and Ann McMillan Harms

A contribution from the proceeds of this book is being made to fund field trips for Memphis schoolchildren to the National Civil Rights Museum.

For my family.   J. C.

For all the children I've taught or learned from over the years, especially Birch.   A. M. H.

Dear Dr. King,

I have a *dream* that I will try my best at school to make good grades and go to college. I have a *dream* that kids won't carry guns or knives anymore. I have a *dream* that everyone will be treated equal. I just want to say to you, Dr. Martin Luther King, Jr., we all *love* you very much.

Yours truly,
Erica, age 13

5

DEAR DR. KING

This poem is my way of asking you a very important question.
The question is: Why did you sacrifice your life?
And why did you feel you were the one
God was calling?

Why?

Why did you not declare war?

Some people think you were a bore!

I know you wanted equal laws,

And it really was a worthy cause.

But why did you have to lose your life?

And leave your children and your wife.

I know they're glad you helped the world,

But what about your sons and your little girls?

They have to go on without your touch,

I know this hurts them very much.

Imagine how they felt that day,

When you were shot and went away.

Still you are a hero in their eyes,

And none could be a bigger prize.

Curiously, Jacinta, age 12

Dear Dr. King,
I wish you were here
because it used to be
White killing Black, now
it's Black killing Black.
If only you were here to
stop violence, because
a girl just died. She just
had 16 years of her life.
If you were here I don't
think there would be
killing like it is.
Every night I go to sleep
praying to see tomorrow.
People down here are
dying like roaches.
Yours truly,
Starkesha, age 11

Dr. King is stopped
by police at
Medgar Evers's funeral.
Jackson, Mississippi,
June, 1963.

Dear Dr. King,

I want to

know if there is a

reason for violence.

Because if there is,

I want to know.

Your friend,

Andrew, age 8

Dear Dr. King,
I am sorry you got shot.
I am glad you decided
to do boycotts, marches,
and sit-ins instead of
violence. I'm glad you
got the Nobel Peace
Prize. Now the man who
shot you is in jail and
will be in jail for a lot of
years to come. I would
have hated the Jim Crow
laws too if I lived back
then.
Your friend,
Becca, age 8

Dear Dr. King,

Hi, my name is Ashley. I'm 11, crazy, funny. I love my class.
I'm in 6th grade. I'm mature, but not that mature.
I still act immature.
I love my family. We have fun on every holiday,
even on your birthday.
My mother is Black. Daddy is half White, half Black.
I work hard. I hardly get into trouble.
Quiet, nice, kind, tenderhearted, and neat.
My neighborhood is not safe
since gangs are coming in the country.
I can't even walk down the street unless my dad comes.
I wish you were still here to help teach our young children
how bad gangs are to our neighborhoods and country.
You were a wonderful peacemaker.
I hope we continue to have great men like you in our country.

Respectfully,
Ashley, age 11

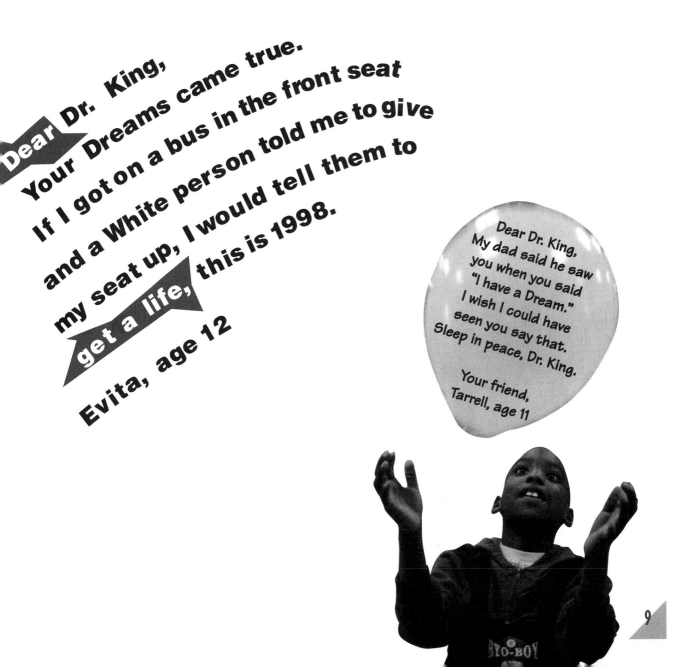

Dear Dr. King,
Your Dreams came true.
If I got on a bus in the front seat
and a White person told me to give
my seat up, I would tell them to
get a life, this is 1998.

Evita, age 12

Dear Dr. King,
My dad said he saw
you when you said
"I have a Dream."
I wish I could have
seen you say that.
Sleep in peace, Dr. King.

Your friend,
Tarrell, age 11

Dear Dr. King,

I am most thankful for what you did for the world. If it was not for you, maybe we would still be getting hosed down with
f i r e h o s e s
and beaten by policemen. But I'm sad to tell you that the
W h i t e s
are not hurting us as much as they were then. Now, Blacks have turned on one another. Young Black men are turning to
g a n g s.
Gangs are responsible for most deaths on Blacks.

Dr. King, guns have helped fill America with violence and
h a t e.
Guns are the leading cause of death right now. Gangsters
g e t g u n s
and shoot who they don't like. America has become all
a b o u t d e a t h.

Sincerely,
Derrick, age 11

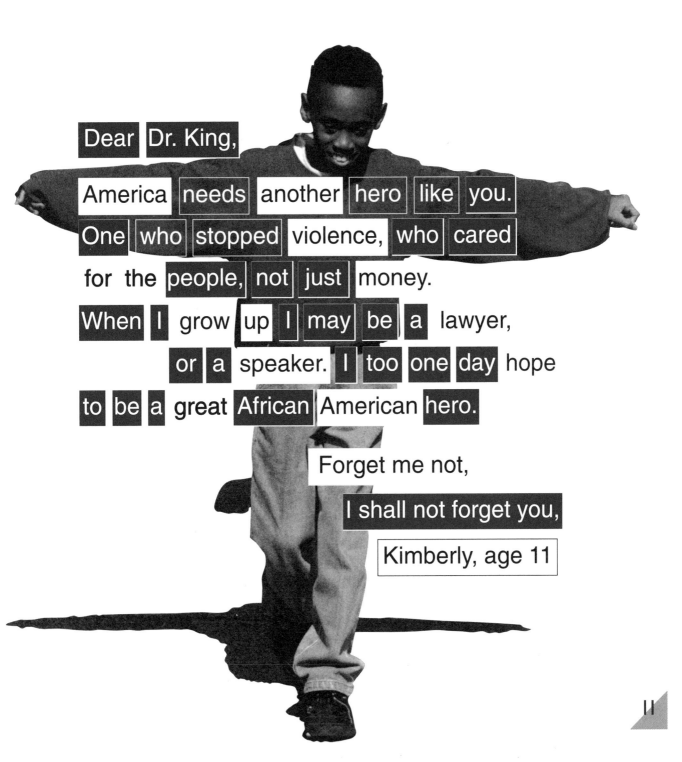

Dear Dr. King,

America needs another hero like you. One who stopped violence, who cared for the people, not just money. When I grow up I may be a lawyer, or a speaker. I too one day hope to be a great African American hero.

Forget me not,

I shall not forget you,

Kimberly, age 11

11

DEAR DR. KING,

IF YOU WERE ALIVE TODAY YOU WOULD GO INTO SHOCK. SOME PEOPLE ARE SCARED TO GO FOR A WALK IN THEIR OWN NEIGHBORHOODS. THEY ARE ALSO SCARED BECAUSE OF DRIVE-BY SHOOTINGS. KIDS ARE ALSO DROPPING OUT OF SCHOOL. THEY THINK SCHOOL IS NOT IMPORTANT. HOW ELSE ARE THEY GOING TO GET A JOB SOMEWHERE ELSE THAN BURGER KING?

I WISH YOU WERE HERE TO HELP THESE PEOPLE.

ERIN, AGE 11

Dear Dr. King,
You made White people hold Black people's hands. I love you, too. You made me happy.
Your friend,
Carmon,
age 9

Dear Dr. King,
Some of the people in my generation don't know how to solve minor problems without weapons or violence. Can you please try to help the people in my generation get back on track so they can grow up right and get an education?

Sincerely,
Pamela,
age 12

Dear Dr. Martin Luther King, Jr.,
My dad said he remembers when he couldn't go to certain places because he was Black. Now he can because of you.

Sincerely,
Krystal, age 10

Dear Dr. King,
I am glad that you studied Gandhi because if you did not I don't think you would be as nice as you were. If you were not even born it would be a violent world and a bloody world, too. I am so glad you were born.

Your friend,
Erin, age 8

Dear Doctor King,
My grandmother, grandfather, uncle, and my father went to your last march. My father told me that they started to throw tear bombs. My father got lost in the crowd but, thank goodness, he found his parents.

Your #1 fan, truly thankful,
Julia, age 10

Dear Dr. King,
I wish that people would learn that violence will not take us anywhere positive.

Thank you,
Jazmin, age 11

Dear Dr. King,
What was it like having the KKK on your tail? Could you stop gang violence? I wish I was a leader like you.

Your friend,
Jordan, age 11

Dear Dr. King,
In my neighborhood there are White people, but mostly Black, and I play with both. If I was over the government I would say "Everybody should be treated equally!"

Your friend,
Nikita, age 8

Dear Dr. King,
You helped me learn that Colored children are no different than White children. I don't know how I can repay you.

Love,
Meredith, age 8

13

Dear Dr. King,

I am a Black young girl. I never got to meet you, but I want to tell you thanks. Because of you there are so many things I can do. Dr. King, it is hard for me to write this letter. Tears are falling from my eyes. So many people did not know who you were. I don't know that much, but I know that you are much more than a Black man, than a father, you have become a symbol of freedom.

Your friend,
Vakeena, age 11

P. S.   I consider myself your friend, so goodbye Doc.

Dear Dr. King,

Thank you for doing the things you did. If you hadn't spoken out I wouldn't have friends like Vakeena and Cecilia.

I think the man who shot you was <u>very</u> mean. He didn't know much about how it doesn't matter what you look like, it's how you act. It's like in preschool, once this boy started coming to school and everybody liked him, but one day he came and his face was all burned because he had been in a fire. Everybody started ignoring him and he became sad. So one day me and my friend went over to where he was playing and asked him to play blocks with us. At first he thought we were going to play some awful trick like other kids often did. But once we started playing we had lots of fun! So it is true you can't judge a person by their looks just like you can't judge a book by its cover.

With awe,
Kathryn, age 10

DEAR DR. MARTIN
LUTHER KING, JR.,

I THOUGHT YOUR
SPEECH WOULD DO IT,
BUT IT DIDN'T, BUT YOU
TRIED.

LOVE,
MAGGIE, AGE 7

Dear Martin,

My name is Uteka. I'm 11 years old.

I was shot when I was 8 years old.

I was shot, but unlike you, I survived.

People fought for your birthday to become a national holiday. Everyone and every school celebrates your birthday and Black History Month in February. We had a program at school called "Let's Join Hands For a Better World" in honor of you.

My neighborhood is neat. There's a lady on my street who is 75 years old. She volunteers to have Bible Study every Tuesday at 4:30. Everyone is welcome. She always talks about you.

My country, I'm sorry to say, is getting worse. At first it seemed to be getting a little better. Now it's kids having kids and children killing children. People now aren't going to see reality until it's too late.

I'm sorry you were shot. I would have taken your bullet. I wish you were still alive to tell people what they are doing to each other is wrong. Who are your heroes? — because you are ours.

Sincerely and Love,

Uteka, age 11

To: Martin Luther King, Jr.

Heaven
Hero Street
Cloud No. 8

Dear Dr. King,

I have a lot of things to ask you and tell you.

First of all, I'll tell you a story.

We were driving to New Orleans for Mardi Gras and we got lost

in a neighborhood and my grandfather said,

"Let's get out of here, there's probably lots of Negroes."

I said, "They are not Negroes, they are people just like us."

My grandfather said, "Yeah, just people. People who will shoot us."

I said "African Americans are no different than us."

Now that I have told you a story,

I would like to ask you a question.

What do you think you accomplished? If you were trying

to get Afro-Americans to be treated like White people, you did it.

Sincerely,

Allison, age 10

Dear Dr. King,
I don't think skin color matters at all.
We're all humans.
Every day, I see how some Whites act around me and
I think some are uncomfortable.
On the other hand, some Whites act normal around
me, like my friend Preston.
I think Whites should not act weird around Blacks.

Sincerely,
Derrick, age 9

Dear Martin Luther King, Jr.,
I don't like it when one boy picks on my friend Derrick.

He calls him a chocolate cake. He picks on me too.
Derrick is a Black boy. If it weren't for you, I wouldn't be
his friend or classmate. He is very nice, but he
can be weird.
Derrick is my only friend and the best one anyone could
ever have. I am writing to you because I need your help.
I don't want anyone making fun of Derrick anymore.

What should I do?
Sincerely,
Preston, age 10

DEAR DR. KING,

DEAR DR. KING,

Dear
Dr.
King,
Just as
you stood
on the
"Mountain
Top", one day I
will too.
If I ever have
children, I will let
them know who Dr.
King was and what
he believed in. Like
freedom of speech,
education, and the best
of all, respect.

I wish you
were still alive.
I would have a
long list of
questions to
ask you. Well,
then again, I
know so much
about you
already, I could
write a novel
about you. And
maybe, some-
day, I will.

Yours truly,
Rachel,
age 8

Did you
ever meet
Malcolm X?
If you did, how did
it feel
to meet
someone
of the
same cause but a
different
religion?

Sincerely,
Eddie,
age 12

Sincerely,
Lawrence, age 13
P.S. Rest in Peace. I have a Dream.

Dear Dr. King, Jr.,

Where I live, Blacks and Whites get along just fine. Some Blacks don't get along with Whites just as well. I think that is stupid 'cause Blacks are just colored with the shades of the earth. I am a Black person. There are about two or three Whites that go to our school. I wish there were more so your dream could really come alive.

Sincerely, Alicia, age 11

Dear Dr. King, Before you came Black people used to be down. They didn't know what the dream was. They didn't know who they were. You made them wake up and understand the dream. You preached the dream to the people you loved.
Love, Jasmine, age 10

Dear Dr. King,
I have heard so
much about you.
My mom said
you wanted equal
rights for everyone.
My dad said you
liked children and
taught them how
to solve problems
without hitting.
My teacher said
you won a
prize of money, and
gave all of it back
to work for peace.
I like you, and I wish
I could see you.

Your friend,
Melvin, age 7

DEAR DR. KING,

WAS YOUR TEACHER BLACK OR WHITE? DID YOUR TEACHER LIKE YOU JUST THE SAME?

LOVE, TAKENDRA, AGE 9

Dear Dr. King,

If you were

alive you would

see your dream

come true.

Blacks and

Whites

live together.

But I have a

question:

how did people

treat Indians?

Your friend,

Sanjeev, age 8

DEAR DR. KING,
HOW IS IT UP THERE?
IS GOD BLACK OR WHITE?
DO YOU GROW OLD UP THERE?
DO YOU SING CHRISTMAS SONGS UP IN HEAVEN?
DO YOU EAT ICE CREAM CONES?
DO YOU HAVE BIRTHDAY PARTIES?
IS GEORGE WASHINGTON UP THERE?

YOUR EARTHLING FRIEND,
RASHAD, AGE 8

Dear Dr. King,
    My grandfather was from your generation. Your words made him realize that racism was wrong. Before he died, he made the Neighborhood Christian Center, an organization that helps deprived families, much larger and more effective at helping more people in many ways.
    I am White, but I understand the way Blacks felt in the past because of your famous speech, and kids in fifth grade visit the Civil Rights Museum and the Lorraine Motel in Memphis every year. Because of you, White and Black kids can be best friends. I hope that remains for the rest of our lives.
                                                            Love, Caroline, age 12

Dear Dr. King, You taught us to fight with words, not hands. I'm happy, you won the Nobel Peace Prize because you were right. You believed in Black Americans and so do I. Martavious, age 13

Dear Dr. King,
I still remember you. Also, the things you did.
I know people that are prejudiced. I still try to play with them.
Sincerely,
Sharmila, age 9

Dear Dr. King,

On your birthday every year I will try to gather

all of my family members.

I will ask them
can we have a party every year.

I love your speech.

I wish you were here right now.

I can see how some people are trying to keep your dream alive.

I have an attitude, but I am trying to get better.

I love you.

You will always hold a special place in my heart.

Sincerely,
Andrea, age 9

Dear Dr. King,

I'm an Asian boy and I like to read the news. But every time I look, it's one religion making war with another religion. There's "holy ground" filled with land mines and missile silos. The world is torn apart by prejudice that may lead to World War. Even in the United States, the land of the free, there is hate and segregation. If we had multiple ministers of peace like you the world would be a lot better place. I hope the world doesn't fall apart and instead joins hands in peaceful unity.

We're all hopeful,
John, age 11

Dear Dr. King,

My name is Attiya and I am 11 years old. I am an average student. I'm writing this letter to talk to you and to thank you.

I may be young, but your kindness towards all mankind (no matter what race) and your courage and strength to end segregation, touched my soul and filled my heart with laughter.

Sometimes I wish I could walk down your path of kindness, courage, and understanding, but sometimes I just want to hurt my enemy, yet I know I can't because I'm afraid they might kill me. Writing this letter to you, Dr. King, is making me realize that I can't fight violence back with violence, but you fight it back with kind words and love.

Dr. King, someday I want to be in heaven, living in peace and harmony with everyone, just like you. I have a dream that today I'll try to be peaceful and nonviolent towards others.

Sincerely and peacefully,
Attiya, age 11

Dear Dr. King,
I have many friends, some are Black, some are White, one is Mexican! As you can see, I'm not prejudiced. I have one of your biographies. I read it over and over. I have lots of your photos. I know that you have a hard head.

You may be upset with me because I've been in fights. Though when I can choose, I walk away.

Frankia, age 11

Sanitation workers march outside Clayborn Temple. Memphis, 1968.

Dear Dr. King,

What made you
become a reformer and
a leader?
Was it courage?
Was it power?
What was your real dream?
What made you tell the real
truth?
White people said you lied, but
you didn't.
You told every Black person your
real dream!
For all the things you did in
your life
you are blessed.

Kyle, age 7

Dear Dr. Martin Luther King, Jr.,
Thanks for all you have done.
Your striving for equality touched all
of mankind. Dr. King, your struggle
laid the ground for the future.

Furthermore, a holiday and a
museum are not enough to describe
or honor you. Moreover, all your
words, thoughts, and achievements
fulfill the dream.

On the other hand, there are
still people who are sweltering with
oppression. In addition to that, jobs,
hospitals, and the judicial system
still show injustice toward African
Americans. Then, besides that,
people continue to practice acts of
injustice in America and all around
the world. However, I, Robert, will
always keep the dream, Your Dream.

Robert, age 12

Dear Dr. King,

If you were alive today I would like to honor you for all the hard work you've done for America. I honor the fact that you were trying to make laws fair when you went to jail, got beaten, and risked your life for us. On your birthday, me and my family read your whole speech out loud and sing songs that you sang. What I'm trying to say is that things like the laws have changed since your death. You succeeded in what you wanted to accomplish. I am just sorry you are not here to know. With peace and happiness I want to say, I love you Dr. King in a very special way.

Yours truly, Marsha, age 12

Dear Dr. King,

My grandad marched with you for freedom. He is gone home now, where you are, to tell you the Whites and Blacks are letting freedom ring. That is what you fought for and went to jail for and died for. So would you please do me a favor and tell my grandad and the rest of my people I love them?

Rest in Peace,
Derrick, age 12.

Dear Dr. King, Jr.,

   If you were alive today, I would say "Thank You."
Since you passed away lots of things have changed. Whites
really opened their eyes and stopped holding a grudge
against all Blacks. Some Whites are still hating Blacks.
Most Blacks help this world be what it is today.

   But after a few years Black-on-Black crime began.
There are 10% more Blacks in jail than in school. I came
to school to be somebody — not a nobody.
People kill people over nothing.
I was looking in a newspaper and
I ran upon a story about a boy
who shot his brother over
a pork chop.
I would never hurt anybody
I love over something to eat.

                    Love truly,
                    La Shundra, age 12

Dear Dr. King,

It seems like every day you see some

racially related incident in the paper.

Some are truth, some nontruth, but the real

truth is that your words are living on past

your death, and they are making a difference

for the better. Your words have changed

many lives and many laws.

Thank you

for how

you have changed my life.

Sincerely,

Tristan, age 11

Dear Dr. King,

When it came to telling the truth you
couldn't be fooled. We all learned
from you. It's a shame we didn't
learn more.
Sincerely,
Greg, age 12

Dear Dr. King,

I wish you were still here so I could hear your speeches.

I'm sorry you died in our city.

and walk all over the city with you.

You tried to help us when we needed you.

I would show you our Civil Rights Museum and my school.

Your friend, Zechariah, age 8

Dear Dr. King,

My dream for America is a non-violent world.

No more homeless people on the street.

No more drug dealers on the street.

More love on earth.

More love on earth.

We need more peace.

Your friend, Lamont, age 9

Dear Dr. King,
Though I am White,
sometimes I picture myself
in a nine-year-old Black girl's
shoes. Your kindness
touched my heart.
Sincerely,
Hannah, age 9

Dear Dr. King,

What would you do if someone called you a monkey? One day a different race called me that. It hurt my feelings because they were White and I was Black. Dr. King, what would you do to these people like skinheads, people who don't like Blacks? Do you like White people? I think people overreact when they see a different race. Things have changed. White will marry Black and Black will marry White. Dr. King, thanks for doing what's right. I think you deserve to be alive.

Sincerely,

Julious, age 11

Dear Dr. King,

Dear Dr. King,

I think the White people treated us terrible because we were

One of the things I admire most about you is your ability

not the same color they were. Last year in fourth grade I watched a

to ignore all the threats that were being shouted at you

movie about some people trying to buy cheeseburgers. The woman

when you marched. I would have crumbled. If I had half

said they did not serve Black people there. But they refused to get

your qualities I'd be a better person. I'm glad you kept

up. Then two or four White boys came up there. One boy poured

peace in your mind and love in your heart. Thank you for

hot coffee on one of them. The other one put a cigarette to her face.

making the world a better place.

The Sheriff came in and they got their burgers.

Sincerely,

It was nice talking to you.

Molly, age 11

Sincerely, Lawrence, age 10

Dear Dr. King,

How did you not fight, but stand up for what you believed in? How did you march? Were your feet hurting?

Now we celebrate your birthday as a holiday.

You are a wonderful and kind man.

Your friend,

Cortney, age 10

William Edwin Jones pushes daughter Renee Andrewnetta Jones during protest march on Main Street. Memphis, 1961.

Dear Dr. King,

You have been a very big influence on my life. A few years ago I went to a school with no Black students, so I really never had any Black friends. This year alone I have learned so much about how Blacks struggled years ago, and have made a lot of Black friends from listening to stories about your life.

When I hear the stories it seems very peculiar to hear that Blacks didn't get to sit at the front of the bus, go to a White school, and many other strange things. Now things have changed and we owe it all to you.

Thank you, Dr. Martin Luther King!

Sincerely,
Amber, age 10

The "Little Rock Nine's" first day of school.
Black students are escorted by police in Little Rock, Arkansas, 1957.

Dear Dr. King,

Your "I Have a Dream" speech really changed people's minds. Now we go to the same restroom and drink out of the same water fountains. Blacks can sit anywhere on the bus. I ride it most days going home. People don't go around anymore calling us niggers. I can eat at any restaurant I want to. I am allowed anywhere I go. In movie theaters I can sit anywhere and on any row. No one can boss us around anymore. Like you said, "We are free at last."

Vondria, age 9

Dear Dr. King,
If you didn't make Whites and Blacks friends, I'd never know Girik, Nadia, Vondria, or Tila. You have touched the hearts of us all around the world, because I'm part of the Jewish culture and without you I would never be at this school right now.

Sincerely,
Sam, age 9

Dear Dr. King,
How did you feel when people were mean to your family? I would surely be mad. What did you do when you were a man and Whites called you "boy"? Were you mad? I wish I got to see you.

Love,
Patrick, age 9

Dear Dr. King,
If you were alive right now, I think you would be proud. You could walk into a school and Black and White children would be playing and talking and eating together. You could walk into a store and if you got thirsty, you could drink from a water fountain that, if marked anything, would have to say "everybody."

Sometimes I think about all you did for us and how little we, Whites, did for you. You might think, "Oh, I only helped Blacks." But you didn't. You helped make Black and White, ages one to one hundred and on past that, friends, which is important.

Thank You,
Sarah, age 10

Dear Dr. Martin Luther King, Jr.,

Thank you for helping stop racism.

You were very brave to lead

all those marches

(especially in the streets).

I can't believe you survived going to jail 3 times.

I'm mad at that dumb White man who shot you.

When I heard that part in the stories

I had to go into my shirt because

I didn't want to show my tears.

Love,
Kyle, age 8

Today after my class went outside we came in and we were allowed to drink from the same water fountain — **all because of you.** We got to work on the computers together — **all because of you.** We went to lunch together and sat at the same table and stood in the same line and ate the same lunches — **all because of you.** Thank you, Dr. King, you changed the world.

Your friend,

Scott, age 12

Dear Dr. King,
When we watched
a video on you
in Social Studies class,
I was stunned at your
power and authority
and how many people
looked up to you.
I look up to you and
wonder what it was
like to be such
an awesome man.
Respectfully,
Gene, age 12

Dear Dr. King,
Things have changed a lot
since you were alive.
Blacks and Whites can
share everything now.
If not, I wouldn't be born.

Sincerely,

Jillian, age 9

Dear Dr. King,

I believe that it is wrong to judge by race. I have known and seen many races in my ten years of living, and even when I die, I will die

believing that I'm not going to let racism stop me from what I can and cannot do.

I also know that I am who I am and if someone doesn't like me because of race, then it's just gonna have to pass me by. I am inspired by you.

I believe if we want to do something, go for it. Do not let racism or anything stop you.

Sincerely,
Reina, age 11

Dear Dr. Martin Luther King, Jr.,

Did you like being a peace-maker?

I will always remember how you made peace in this country, and I will tell my children.

Sincerely,
Evan, age 8

Protest marchers on Main Street. Memphis, 1961.

BECAUSE I WANT EQUALITY WHILE I AM YOUNG I VE BEEN JAIL R ATTEMPTIN PUT RACY

DON'T BUY HERE We Too Can TYPE SPELL AND COUNT!

N.A.C.P.

Civil Rights = in '61 = Don't Wait 'Till I'm Sixty-One!

NAACP

Dear Dr. Martin Luther King, Jr.,

My friend is a racist, and she wants me to be one, too. My friend really needs a lot of help. Carmen, age 10

Dear Dr. King,

We could sure use your help nowadays. Not only has segregation between Blacks and Whites started again, but now some people are rude in helping people of their own color. For example, many of the handicapped and disabled children only have each other, because people think they have something that others can catch and it caused them to become that way. Children in schools pick their friends, and many of the "strange ones," as they would put it, don't get picked.

Overton Park Zoo. One day a week was designated for Blacks only. Memphis, 1950s.

There are a lot more problems than just segregation in our world today. About one person, at least, in a city dies each day. Many of them die from drive-by shootings and robberies. Children's foster homes are full, because young women decide to abandon their children on the streets, and it is so hard to find kind people to adopt them. Many don't even care. It's a sad world today, very sad.

Kimberly,
age 11

Dear Dr. King,
I love you because you made the world better because the White and Black people couldn't be friends and play and you made it so they can play together always.
I want to ask you,
are there Black and White angels in heaven?
I think they play together, too.
Love, Morgan, age 6

Dear Dr. King,
   I like to play with other people. I try to say "stop" when they're fighting.
Brown and White children are going to school together. It's like we are in the same tribe.
The world has changed a lot.
              Love, Angela, age 8

Dear Dr. King,

It is disturbing to think that good people can be killed so brutally. You fought so hard for what was right. If you walk down a hall this month, Black History Month, in our school, you can see clusters of silhouettes of the most interesting and fascinating people, that includes yourself. You would be pleased to know that every child in this school knows all about your doings. Even my second grade brother is getting interested in Black history.

We still have racism, no there is no stopping that, a demon who burns fire in the hearts of men, so terrible. I hate to think of what might have happened if you hadn't been around. I have a friend in my class named Brandon. He is Black. To know that children just thirty years ago could have been prevented the joy of knowing such nice people is a sad thought. Your thoughts and ideals are being carried out by children and adults all across the world. I just hope that whatever good news I can tell you can make a warm smile spread across that face we have come to know as a symbol of peace and brotherhood.

Dear Dr. Martin Luther King, Jr.,

Yes, gone is most of the open segregation and violence. No one is killed when they go to vote. Everybody can ride on the same bus. However, segregation continues where it's hard to see. At schools, Black and White children trade insults. Asians are cheated at the supermarket. White people and Blacks live in different neighborhoods. Government has abolished most public segregation, but segregation still lives. We need to carry on your dream, or things may just get worse.

Sincerely, Leath, age 11

Dear Martin Luther King,
I was amazed to find out that you walked with people from city to city to help stop prejudice. I thought that was wonderful. I was also shocked that you never fought back violently or raised your voice. If I were you, to be honest, I would have probably taken a swing at them!
Sincerely,
Virginia,
age 11

**Protest marches after assassination of Dr. King.
Main and Madison Streets, Memphis, 1968.**

Dear Dr. King,

I wanted to ask you, didn't you get angry when people yelled, screamed, and threw rocks and dirt at you? Every time I saw you in a book you were so bright and happy. Were you ever sad?

Martin, I know how you felt because when I was in kindergarten I fell off my bike and landed on my head and I had to have brain surgery and all my friends betrayed me after surgery because I had a half head of hair. I felt so angry. Martin, how come you didn't lose your temper?

Sincerely, Willy, age 11

Dear Dr. King,
     Did they have Nintendos back then?
Was it cool talking to John F. Kennedy?
                              From, Thomas, age 8

Dear Dr. King,
     Your dream became a real thing.
I've seen many arguments that people have had
so I told them about your dream. My brother has had
many arguments with people who are Colored. So I just
go over to a tree and think about your dream.
                              Yours sincerely, Janie, age 7

Dear Dr. King,
     We have gangs in our neighborhood. People are always killing
other people. Some are killing themelves. People can't stop,
they just go on and on killing themselves.
     When I grow up and get married, I want my husband to be just like you.
                              Yours truly, Tamara, age 11

Dear Dr. King,
Just remember this:

Roses are **red**,

Violets are **blue**,

You freed **America**,

And **Lincoln** helped, too.

I've always wondered if you had a sense of humor.
You probably do, but I don't know.

Sincerely, Becky, age 9

Dear Dr. Martin Luther King, Jr.,
    Rebecca is my friend. She is White.
But all my classmates make fun of her and it makes her cry
inside and it makes her mad inside. Stephanie and I cheer her up.
So Dr. King, I wish you could make the bad kids act better.

Your friend, Yolanda, age 9

Dear Dr. King,
Did you have verbs when you were in school?

Love, Tawanda, age 9

Dear Dr. King,

The racial stuff doesn't matter now.
You've changed American ways. Your braveness
and open heart are remembered in every American's heart.
You're famous for honesty
and trueness.

We love you dearly.

Sincerely,

Sally, age 7

Dear Dr. King,
My friends Trevor and Claudius
have been fighting.
Can you help them stop fighting?
Trevor got hit in his eye and he cried.

From your friend,
Bradley, age 7

P.S. I hope you had a good birthday.

Dear Dr. King,
I think the trick was good when you and other African Americans didn't ride the bus to work. You rode some cars, like a carpool, to work so you could sit where you want on the bus.
    Sincerely,
    Mark, age 9

DEAR DR. KING,
I WISH YOU WERE STILL ALIVE TO SEE THE ADVANCEMENTS OF BLACK PEOPLE. WE HAVE MORE PEOPLE INVOLVED IN THE GOVERNMENT. WE ALSO HAVE OUR OWN BUSINESSES AND WE ARE TREATED EQUALLY LIKE YOU DREAMED WE WOULD BE. YOU ARE A TRUE BLACK HERO.
    SINCERELY,
    LOUIS, AGE 12

DEAR DR. KING,
I AM NOT BLACK OR WHITE. DID THEY MAKE INDIAN COLOR HAVE SEPARATE STUFF TOO? WITHOUT YOU WE WOULDN'T HAVE THE STUFF WE HAVE TODAY BECAUSE A LOT OF BLACK PEOPLE INVENTED THE STUFF WE HAVE TODAY.
    YOURS TRULY,
    GIRIK, AGE 8

Dear Dr. King,
I wanted to ask you: what was it like struggling and striving to survive and help people? I feel that you did right by coming to Memphis to help the sanitation workers. How else would they be paid better?
    Your friend,
    Charla, age 12

Dear Dr. King,

WE ARE NO MORE CALLED COLORED. WE NOW ANSWER TO "AFRICAN AMERICAN" AND I AM PROUD OF IT. MY MOM SAID SHE REMEMBERED WHEN IT WAS BLACK HISTORY WEEK. SOME PEOPLE WENT ON AND CHANGED THAT AND NOW IT IS BLACK HISTORY MONTH. I KEEP ON SAYING TO MYSELF, WHY A WEEK OR A MONTH FOR ALL OUR ACHIEVEMENTS? WE EARNED A WHOLE DECADE! I AM GOING TO FOLLOW ALL MY BLACK ANCESTORS' FOOTSTEPS. I'LL BE A STRONG BLACK LEADER AND ACHIEVE MORE.

I WOULD HAVE LOVED FOR YOU TO BE OUT AT THE MILLION MAN MARCH. IT WOULD REALLY SEND OUT THE MESSAGE TO ALL THE PEOPLE AND NOT JUST BLACKS.

Sincerely,
JONATHAN, AGE 12

Dear Dr. King,

We need you back.

Our world is
falling apart!

Gang violence needs to stop.
Our people are killing each other
and selling drugs.
Young people are getting guns
and getting shot.
One day me and my friends were
riding our bikes and we rode
past a White boy's house.
We didn't say anything to him,
but he called us "NIGGERS."
My friends went back
and said something to him,
but I went home.
The reason I went home was
because I knew who I was
and not what he wanted me to be.
These are just a few of the reasons
we need you back for good!

Sincerely, Jarvis, age 12

Sanitation workers assemble for a solidarity march.
This was Dr. King's last march. Memphis, March 28, 1968.

Dear Dr. King,

In Music, my class and I are singing songs

about you. Why would the police put

someone who is working for peace in jail?

I hope you hear the angels sing about

your dream coming alive.

Sincerely, Lillian, age 7

Dear Dr. King,
Maybe if you were here today you would be happy,
maybe not. There is no
segregation, but there is
racism and hate. I must live
with much racism in my
family, my neighborhood,
and our world. I cannot
understand why people
cannot let go of their weapons and, instead,
hold each other's hands.
You had a dream that turned into a nightmare
and you lost your life.

Sincerely,
Hailey, age 11

Dear Dr. King,

I wish that your dream could come true. You would not believe how things are going nowadays. Our own people are killing each other. Dr. King, this is the time that we need you the most, although we understand that you cannot be here to help us through these trials and tribulations.

We also understand that you have done all you could for us on this earth. Now I think we should take charge and make this world a better place for all of us. I know, Dr. King, that one day freedom will ring. I also know that one day we will sit down at that table of brotherhood. I know, Dr. King, that one day we will sing that old Negro spiritual "free at last, free at last, thank God almighty, we're free at last."

Cortez, age 13

P.S. We shall overcome someday.

Dear Dr. King,

My dream is to have a peaceful world. I always wonder as I go to school in the morning and as I come home from school if I will make it home to see another day. Sometimes when I look out of the window I think about how beautiful the sky is and if I will ever live to see fifty years old. Because the world is so cruel today that you have to watch out wherever you go. Every night you hear gunshots and every night another Black dies. Sometimes I wish I had been living in the 1960s.

Well, thank you for everything you did. It worked out. The Whites aren't on the Blacks anymore. Now it's Blacks on Blacks. And I surely wish it would stop.

Sincerely,

Claudia, age 11

Marchers include Malcolm Blackburn, Pastor of Clayborn Temple, during sanitation workers' strike. Memphis, 1968.

Dear Dr. King,

I'm mad that you are dead. But I'm glad that you did that march to freedom. I'm especially glad that you ran that boycott, because Rosa Parks didn't have to get out of that seat. Because she paid to ride that bus, so she sat where she wanted to sit. In these days, Whites and Blacks are friends and families. If it weren't for you we would still not be equal.

Your friend,

Devario, age 13

DEAR DR. KING,

MY FRIEND ASHLEY IS BLACK AND I AM WHITE.
WE LIKE BEING FRIENDS.
SHE IS MY BEST FRIEND AND I WOULDN'T HAVE IT ANY
OTHER WAY.
I LIKE BEING NEAR HER.

I LIVE NORTH OF MEMPHIS, TENNESSEE, WHERE
YOU DIED.
MY FRIENDS ARE PEOPLE WHO ARE RESPECTABLE AND GOOD STUDENTS.
I LOVE TO READ. I LIKE TO SING.
I SOMETIMES WONDER WHY TEENAGERS ARE SO DISRESPECTFUL.
I SEE THEM ALL THE TIME.
I BET MOTHERS GET THEIR
HEARTS BROKEN.

YOU ARE MY HERO AND
FOREVER MORE YOU WILL BE.

SINCERELY,
MEGAN, AGE 10

Dear Dr. King,

Today we celebrate your birthday every year on January 15th. We also have a program for Black History Month. Kids, Black and White, study for weeks on this one play. We do speeches and dances. Also, kids don't go to school on that day. We have a fundraiser called United Way to help the poor, Black and White, and buy them food to eat.

Things have changed some while you have been gone. Blacks and Whites are going out with each other, making babies together, best friends. We go to the same school. We go to the same doctor's office. We drink from the same water fountain.

In 1994 a man was killed in our front yard. Three girls, Chinese, White, and Black, trying to get in a gang stabbed him about seven times. They wrapped the knife and laid it in our front yard.

Sincerely,

Crystal, age 11

Dear Dr. King,

You were fair.

And you knew right from wrong.

I am sorry you were dragged into jail.

You cared for people.

And you were a true person.

I am sorry you got shot.

God believed in you.

Your friend,
Liam, age 6

Dear Dr. King,
My parents are from India, an[d]
Gandhi made a humongous
difference in their lives like you
have made in mine.
You are another Gandhi in my lif[e]

Yours truly,
Anu[n]... 10

Dear Dr King,
I have two problems.
One: Some workers are cutting down trees and families live in them.
Two: Pizza people don't come around any more because of our skin.
Tell me what to do.
Tell me why.
Love,
Brittany, age 7

Dear Dr. Martin Luther King, Jr.,
Last year on the news I heard about a little boy who brought a gun to school. I want to know what you would do or say to the young boy. A few years ago I heard about some young men, Black and White, that robbed an old lady's house. What I am wondering is if one of these people were in your family and did this would you still love this person like you always did or would you not even want to talk to him/her?
        Your admirer,
        Tiffany, age 10

Dear Dr. King,

It would have been

a lost world if you

didn't come into it.

There is still a lot

of violence going

on here.

If you can, please

send someone down

from heaven to help.

Sincerely, Ellen, age 9

Dear Dr. King,

I know that we have come a long way

but we still have a long way to go.

Mule train leaves for Washington, D.C., as part of the Poor People's March.
Marks, Mississippi, 1968.

I think that most of your dream has come true

and I think that your children are being judged by

the content of their character

and not by their skin color.

Sincerely,

William, age 12